FRONTLINE FAMILIES

WORLD WAR I

Frontline Soldiers and Their Families

Nick Hunter

Gareth Stevens
PUBLISHING

Please visit our website, **www.garethstevens.com**. For a free color catalog of all our high-quality books, call toll free 1-800-542-2595 or fax 1-877-542-2596.

Library of Congress Cataloging-in-Publication Data

Hunter, Nick.
World War I: frontline soldiers and their families / by Nick Hunter.
p. cm. — (Frontline families)
Includes index.
ISBN 978-1-4824-3065-3 (pbk.)
ISBN 978-1-4824-3068-4 (6 pack)
ISBN 978-1-4824-3066-0 (library binding)
1. World War, 1914-1918 — Juvenile literature.
2. World War, 1914 - 1918 — Social aspects — Juvenile literature.
I. Hunter, Nick. II. Title.
D522.7 H86 2016
940.3—d23

First Edition

Published in 2016 by
Gareth Stevens Publishing
111 East 14th Street, Suite 349
New York, NY 10003

© 2016 Gareth Stevens Publishing

Produced by Calcium
Editors for Calcium: Sarah Eason and Rachel Warren Chadd
Designers: Paul Myerscough and Jessica Moon
Picture researcher: Susannah Jayes

Cover: Wikipedia Commons: Private Jim Rae; Inside: Shutterstock: Natasha Breen 14, Susan Law Cain 4, 10, 12, 40, Everett Collection 26, 38, Igor Golovniov 15tr, 44, Jeff Gynane 19b, Harris & Ewing 23, LiliGraphie 18, 28t, Jason Maehl 43b; Willequet Manuel 43t, Photoiconix 13, Elena Ray 7, Elzbieta Sekowska 19t, Slava2009 31, TonLammerts 21t, Max Voran 23b, Wikimedia Commons: 22, 39, Archiv Corps Masovia 29, Australian War Museum 17, British Library 25, City of Toronto Archives 41, Guy de Rambaud 15, Imperial War Museums 8, Jefferson Parish Library Archives 37, Library of Congress 6, 23, 30, 32, 33, 36, National Archives and Records Administration 21t, 35, 42, National Library of France 27, National Library of Scotland 24, PD-BritishGov 5b, Private Jim Rae 1, The India & Colonial Exhibition 5t, United Kingdom Government 34.

Printed in the United States of America
CPSIA compliance information: Batch #CS15GS: For further information contact Gareth Stevens, New York, New York at 1-800-542-2595.

CHAPTER 1

WORLD WAR I

In the summer of 1914, Europe was plunged into a devastating war that would claim millions of lives and last for more than four years. This conflict, which people at the time called the Great War, did not just change the lives of the millions of men who fought in it. It also had a big impact on families and children who were often far from the front line.

A Global Conflict

The war was fought between Germany and Austria-Hungary on one side, which faced the combined armies of Great Britain, France, Russia, and their allies. As the conflict went on, other countries were dragged into it. Fighting spread to Asia and Africa. In 1917, the United States finally joined the war on the side of Great Britain, France, and their allies. It was now truly a world war.

Allied soldiers fighting bloody trench battles on the Western Front were later joined by US ground forces who helped to secure the final victory.

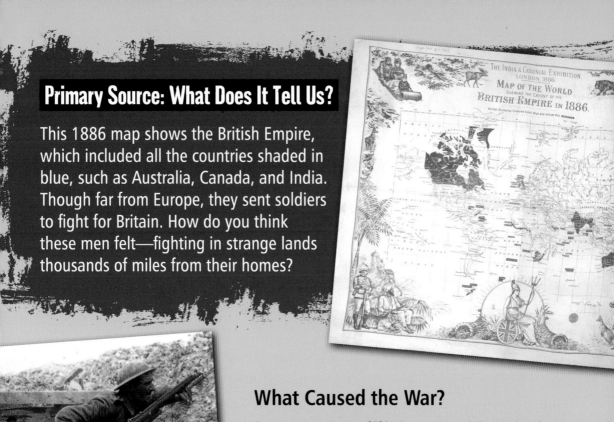

Primary Source: What Does It Tell Us?

This 1886 map shows the British Empire, which included all the countries shaded in blue, such as Australia, Canada, and India. Though far from Europe, they sent soldiers to fight for Britain. How do you think these men felt—fighting in strange lands thousands of miles from their homes?

THE INDIA & COLONIAL EXHIBITION
LONDON 1886
MAP OF THE WORLD
SHEWING THE EXTENT OF THE
BRITISH EMPIRE IN 1886.

A British soldier keeps watch from a trench in France.

What Caused the War?

For a century before 1914, the nations of Europe had lived mostly in peace with each other, but rivalries and jealousies had built up. Prussia and many smaller states had united to form the mighty German Empire. Germany was a rival, not only to her neighbor France but also to the British Empire. Russia and Austria-Hungary were competing for power in Eastern Europe, but smaller countries, such as Serbia and Bosnia-Herzegovina, wanted to rule themselves.

When Archduke Franz Ferdinand, heir to the throne of Austria-Hungary, was shot by Serbian nationalists on June 28, 1914, the complex system of alliances and rivalries meant that, within a few weeks, most of Europe was at war.

A CHANGING WORLD

During World War I, life changed dramatically for families. Men left their families behind to prepare for battle, and women began working in jobs formerly carried out by men. This meant that many families were separated for long periods of time, and their lives changed forever.

Changes to Family Life

The war meant that children's fathers were away on the front line and their mothers now worked in jobs away from the home—often in military factories where they helped make ammunition for soldiers fighting in the war. With all efforts focused on sending supplies to the front line, certain foods, such as those made from wheat, were less available to families. Women had to change the way they worked, and the foods they cooked for their families.

Secondary Source: What Does It Tell Us?

Look at this poster from World War I. It shows a woman cooking with cornmeal, oats, and barley. The wording of the poster reads, "she is doing her part to help win the war." What do you think this means? How might reducing the amount of wheat a family ate have helped the war effort? Explain your thinking.

she is doing her part to help win the war

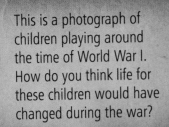

This is a photograph of children playing around the time of World War I. How do you think life for these children would have changed during the war?

Wartime Childhood

Life for children became very different during World War I, compared with how it had been before the war. Children became responsible for many of the jobs that their mothers would previously have done at home. There was much less time to play because there were now many more daily chores to do.

Not only did the day-to-day lives of children in wartime families become physically harder, the children themselves became emotionally tougher, too. They had to deal with the threat that their fathers and brothers could be injured or even killed in battle. Families dreaded the arrival of a message by telegram or mail that told them that a father, brother, uncle, or cousin on the front line had been injured or killed.

This is a summary of the main events of World War I. In the West, the longest phase was the four years of devastating trench warfare before the final Allied victory.

1914

June 28: Assassination of Archduke Franz Ferdinand, heir to the throne of Austria-Hungary. Austria-Hungary blames Serbia and threatens military action.

July 28–August 4: Major powers of Europe declare war on each other. Germany and Austria-Hungary take up arms against France, Great Britain, Russia, and Belgium.

Early September: First Battle of the Marne, near Paris, halts German invasion of France, and trench warfare begins on the Western Front.

October 29: Ottoman Empire (modern Turkey) enters the war on the same side as Germany and Austria-Hungary.

1915

January 19: First zeppelin raid on Britain.

April: Allied forces land at Gallipoli in the Dardanelles, northwestern Turkey. They are evacuated in January 1916 after heavy casualties.

May 7: RMS *Lusitania* sunk by torpedo from German submarine with loss of 1,198 lives.

PUBLIC WARNIN

The public are advised to familiarise themselves with the appe of British and German Airships and Aeroplanes, so that they ma be alarmed by British aircraft, and may take shelter if Ge aircraft appear. **Should hostile aircraft be seen**, take s **immediately** in the nearest available house, preferably in the base and remain there until the aircraft have left the vicinity: do not s about in crowds **and do not touch unexploded bombs.**

In the event of **HOSTILE** aircraft being seen in country districts, the nearest Naval, Military or Authorities should, if possible, be advised immediately by Telephone of the TIME OF APPEARANC DIRECTION OF FLIGHT, **and whether the aircraft is an Airship or an Aeroplane.**

GERMAN	BRITISH
AIRSHIPS	AIRSHIPS
AEROPLANES	AEROPLANES

Note specially the shape of the Airships and the position of the passenger cars

Note specially the sloped-back wings of the German Aeroplanes

This British poster tells people how to prepare for enemy air attacks.

May 23: Italy joins the war on the side of Britain, France, and Russia.

September: Major Allied attack launched at Loos, on the Western Front.

1916

February 21: Battle of Verdun begins in France—one of the bloodiest battles of the war.

May 31: In the North Sea, Battle of Jutland begins between British and German navies.

July 1: Start of the Battle of the Somme on the Western Front. Almost 60,000 British troops are killed or wounded on the first day.

1917

February 1: Germany declares unrestricted submarine warfare, threatening to sink without warning any ships supplying the Allies, even if they are from the neutral United States.

March 8: Beginning of Russian Revolution, which deposes Czar Nicholas II and throws Russia's war effort into chaos.

April: Wave of mutinies and strikes by French soldiers and workers protesting against the war.

April 6: United States declares war on Germany.

May 18: Selective Services Act introduces conscription (draft) in the United States.

July 31: Start of the Battle of Passchendaele, near Ypres, Belgium.

December 9: Allied forces in the Middle East capture Jerusalem.

1918

March 3: Russia's new government agrees peace with Germany in Treaty of Brest-Litovsk, giving up large areas of territory in Eastern Europe and freeing up German forces to concentrate on the Western Front.

March 21: Germany launches major attack on Western Front, forcing Allied forces to retreat.

May: First American forces in action on the Western Front, led by General John Pershing. By this time, around 500,000 American troops are stationed in France.

July: British, French, and US armies begin major offensives (attacks) on the Western Front.

September: Allied forces reach Germany's defensive Hindenburg Line. Within a few weeks, Germany seeks to end the war.

November 11: Armistice agreed to end fighting between Germany and the Allies. Austria-Hungary had already signed an armistice a few days earlier.

CHAPTER 2

FIGHTING THE WAR

World War I was not only the first global war—it was also the first major conflict to be fought on land, sea, and in the air. Vast land armies faced each other on the battlefields of Europe. Land troops also fought in the very different terrain of Africa and the Middle East. For the first time, aircraft were used to attack enemy troops and civilians.

Major Battle Areas

The main battle zones were the Western and Eastern Fronts in Europe. After Germany's initial invasion of Belgium and northern France, the Western Front hardly moved until 1918.

Most American troops fought on the Western Front during 1918.

Yanks going into action France

It was made up of hundreds of miles of trenches, stretching from France's border with Switzerland up to the North Sea. The Eastern Front was longer and more changeable, as Russians, Germans, and Austrians battled across the lands of Eastern Europe. Some towns in the east were fought over several times during the course of the war, as one side or the other gained the upper hand.

The War at Sea

Control of the sea routes to Europe was still vital for both sides, although the Battle of Jutland in 1916 was the only major naval battle of the war. From the beginning of the war, Britain used its navy to prevent food and supplies reaching Germany and Austria-Hungary. This may have helped the Allies win the war, but it also led to terrible food shortages for families in Central Europe, causing hundreds of thousands of deaths from starvation.

Germany used submarines–called U-boats–to keep ships from reaching Britain and France. Hundreds of ships were sunk by submarines. Many of them were carrying food and war supplies such as ammunition, but ships also brought troops to Europe from as far away as Australia, New Zealand, and the United States.

Air Power

In 1914, aircraft were still just a few years old, but they were soon adapted for use in wartime. Both sides used airplanes to gather information on enemy trenches and troop movements. They were also used to bomb trenches and fight each other in the air. Aircraft technology was still very new, and being a pilot was one of the most dangerous jobs of the war.

When war broke out in August 1914, the German army did all it could to win a quick victory against France. To achieve this, the army invaded neutral Belgium, which led to Britain declaring war. After weeks of bloody battles, the German advance was halted at the Battle of the Marne, near Paris. German forces defended their positions by digging trenches that would protect them from enemy artillery and machine gun fire.

In the years that followed, armies tried heroically to break through the enemy's line of trenches. Hundreds of thousands of men were killed and wounded in terrible confrontations such as the Battle of Verdun and the Battle of the Somme in 1916. Between the battles, soldiers had to deal with constant danger, cold, and boredom.

Trench Life

There were usually three or more lines of trenches on each enemy's side, connected by communication trenches. Soldiers would spend a few days at a time in the frontline trench, but spent more time in support trenches, living in underground shelters or dugouts.

This postcard from the Front shows Salvation Army volunteers making doughnuts. Usually, food was unappetizing and, during battles, it was very scarce.

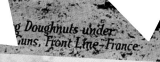

g Doughnuts under
uns, Front Line, France

This reconstruction shows what the trenches of World War I looked like.

Writing letters home was one way for soldiers to defeat the boredom of their lives. In most of these letters soldiers said little about what trench life was really like–to protect their families from the reality of warfare. Trenches were infested with rats and lice. Soldiers were also aware of the constant danger–they or their friends could instantly be shot by a sniper's bullet if they stuck their heads aboveground.

Primary Source: What Does It Tell Us?

To fight overseas in 1914, by law British soldiers had to be 19, but many younger men claimed to be older so that they could join the war. This short note was written by Stephen Brown,* who was stationed in France in December 1914. How do you think he was feeling when he wrote the letter?

*Stephen was killed on the Western Front a few months later, in May 1915.

Dear Mother

Just a line to let you know that I am quite well. I am for the Front on Tuesday. But if you write to the Commanding Officer and say I am only seventeen, it will stop me from going. Get it here before Tuesday for I cannot get a pass to come and see you. Don't forget.

From Stephen

EASTERN EUROPE

As neither side could make progress on the Western Front, military leaders hoped that Russia's huge army would be able to defeat Germany and Austria-Hungary in the east. The war on the Eastern Front, however, was fought over a much wider area than the war in the West. During the war years, land in Poland and elsewhere was often controlled by one side, then the other. Neither could make a decisive breakthrough when so much of Germany's strength was focused on attacking France and Great Britain in the West.

Russia Under Strain

Russia could mobilize millions of soldiers, but they were often poorly equipped and badly led. As the war developed, some did not even have rifles or warm clothes to cope with the bitter winter weather.

The war also took many Russian farm laborers away from their families and the land they farmed. Without them, food production collapsed and hunger became a problem for the women and children left behind, as well as for the men on the front line. Many families in land controlled by Austria-Hungary also faced hunger, as a blockade by the British and French navies kept food from reaching Central Europe.

Almost 1.5 million Austro-Hungarian soldiers died in the war, and thousands of civilians had died of starvation by 1918.

Left: Czar Nicholas II (on the left) was Russia's all-powerful ruler. He understood little of the grinding poverty most of his people lived in.

Millions of troops were taken prisoner on the Eastern Front. They relied on food being sent from home and, as food shortages began to take hold, prisoners of war often did not have enough to eat.

Above: Fighting on the Eastern Front took its toll on families; thousands of people died of starvation.

Families Under Fire

Ordinary families suffered as a direct result of fighting on the Eastern Front. When Russian forces retreated across Poland in 1915, many thousands of Polish families were forced to leave their homes.

One country that suffered more than almost any other was Serbia. Austria-Hungary's attack on Serbia was the first action of the war, but this small country in the Balkans did not give in easily. Serbian resistance held out, although men, women, and children were massacred by the invaders. Serbia was finally invaded by German and Bulgarian armies in December 1915. More than one-quarter of the country's population was killed or wounded in the war.

Germany, France, and especially Great Britain controlled lands outside the borders of Europe. These colonies were soon dragged into the war as British forces, which included Indian and African troops, seized African lands that Germany had controlled. Fighting in the hot, humid jungles of Africa was very different from the cold and mud of the Western Front. When the Ottoman Empire joined the war in October 1914, Turkish lands in the Middle East also saw military campaigns. US President Woodrow Wilson was determined that the United States would stay neutral.

Attacking Turkey

In 1915, Allied leaders decided to attack Turkey, believing it was weaker than Germany or Austria-Hungary. They launched a daring attack at Gallipoli in the Dardanelles, a narrow part of the Turkish Straits linking the Mediterranean Sea and Black Sea. The attack was a disaster, and many of those who died were soldiers from Australia and New Zealand, fighting thousands of miles from their families.

The War in Africa

The campaigns outside Europe were not just fought by European troops or those who had traveled from places such as Australia. Many Africans were forced to join the war, either as support workers or even as troops. These people had to leave their families, but often had little idea what they were fighting for.

Primary Source: What Does It Tell Us?

Irish soldier Henry Hanna took part in the Gallipoli campaign of 1915. From this 1917 account, how do you think it affected him?

"Then came my dash for safety. I made two rushes of it, and had to shout to our fellows to stop firing to allow me to get in. I got a splinter of a bullet in the side. It just pricked the skin and stuck in my belt. There is a hole in my belt where it stuck .... The sights I saw going along that place I shall never forget. Some of our fellows throwing back the bombs which the Turks threw over, and which had not exploded. Wounded and dead lying everywhere. The sun streaming down, and not a drop of water to be had."

News of disasters like the landing at Gallipoli could take many days to reach families at home, as there was no TV or radio broadcasting.

CHAPTER 3

THE CHANGING ROLE OF WOMEN

World War I was one of the first wars to involve vast conscript armies. Millions of men were drafted into the military and forced to leave their homes, jobs, and families. Even the United States drafted millions of men after joining the war in 1917. With their husbands and sons away fighting the war, many of them returning injured or not at all, women had to take on different roles in society.

A Life-Changing War

Before the war broke out, the lives of women across Europe and North America were very different from those of most women today. Very few had the chance to get the education and training necessary for professional jobs such as doctor or engineer. Many women went to work after leaving school in their early teens, but would stop working when they got married.

Women from wealthy families were not expected to work, but many chose to help the war effort as nurses or ambulance drivers.

There were few labor-saving devices such as refrigerators or washing machines to help women manage housework and their families' needs.

World War I caused big changes in the world of work, as more women began to fill jobs vacated by men who were fighting at the front line. Home life also changed as women had to care for their families without the support of husbands and grown-up sons.

Freedom and Responsibility

For many women, the war actually brought new freedoms, and higher-paid jobs than they had before the war. This was mainly true for those without family responsibilities, although almost everyone had fathers and brothers fighting on the front line. For those with husbands or children, the war brought more responsibility and the problems of juggling work and family. For those whose loved ones were killed, or badly wounded in the war, life would never be the same again.

Most women left their jobs once they were married, but this changed when husbands joined the military.

VOTES for WOMEN

VOTES

FOR

WOMEN

Before the war, women had been campaigning in many countries for the right to vote in elections.

WOMEN AT WORK

Before the war, many women went to work before they were married. Working-class families often depended on the money both parents could earn in factories. Millions of women also worked as cooks, maids, and domestic servants in the houses of wealthy families.

Once war broke out, all the warring countries soon started to employ women in jobs that had been vacated by men serving in the military forces. In France, women worked as conductors on the streetcars. In Britain, women were also employed as drivers on London's buses. Before 1914, it had been unusual for women to work in offices in many countries, but this became common and was a lasting change as a result of the war.

Making Weapons and Ammunition

The warring nations had to supply their frontline forces with huge amounts of artillery shells and bullets to keep the war going. By the end of the war, munitions factories in Britain employed 950,000 women, compared to 700,000 in Germany.

Primary Source: What Does It Tell Us?

Miss C. West worked as a cook at the Woolwich Arsenal in London. In her diary, she talked about the conditions inside a munitions factory. Does this sound like a good place to work? Why did people have to work in such conditions?

"Then I was shown the lyddite works. This is a bright canary yellow powder (picric acid) and comes to the factory in wooden tubs. ... The house, (windows, doors, floor, and walls) is bright yellow, and so are the faces and hands of all the workers. As soon as you go in, the powder in the air makes you sneeze and splutter and gives you a horrid bitter taste at the back of the throat."

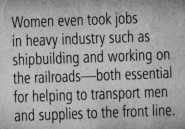

Women even took jobs in heavy industry such as shipbuilding and working on the railroads—both essential for helping to transport men and supplies to the front line.

Demand for Women

In 1917 and 1918, the demand for women workers in these jobs grew in the United States, as men enlisted to fight in the war. Women were in particular demand for office and administrative work. As in Europe, women also began to fill jobs in heavy industry. One newspaper reported that, in just a few months, the number of women working on the Pennsylvania Railroad had more than doubled to nearly 4,000 employees.

Although women were taking over men's jobs, they were usually paid less than male workers. Labor unions often opposed women taking these jobs, and insisted that men would get their jobs back at the end of the war.

Workers in the giant munitions factories, where shells such as this one were made, not only faced the danger of catastrophic explosions. The chemicals they worked with were toxic, turning skin and hair yellow over time.

WORKING ON THE LAND

The supply of food was as important as the supply of gunpowder in winning the war. From 1914, the British navy tried to keep food and supplies from reaching Germany by sea. German U-boats fought back, sinking ships bound for Britain and France. The warring nations in Europe used as much land as they could to grow food, and women had to replace men working on the land.

Women and Farms

Female members of farming communities had always played their part, particularly when the harvest was gathered. As men volunteered to fight, women and children took on a bigger role in running their farms. Later in the war, as men were drafted to serve in the war, and trade blockades started to have an impact, shortage of labor in farming became a major problem. In Britain, the Women's Land Army (WLA) was launched in March 1917. By the end of the war, around 300,000 women were working on farms.

Work on the land was often hard, with many plows still drawn by horses. In Britain, fuel shortages meant that tractors could not always be used even if the farm owned one. Women farmworkers were not organized to the same extent in Germany, which probably made food shortages in Germany and Austria-Hungary even worse.

The WLA provided cheap labor for farmers, who were sometimes unhappy about employing women.

Women's Land Army of America (WLAA) volunteers came from colleges, women's organizations, and gardening clubs.

Women's Land Army of America

Inspired by the British organization, the WLAA was set up by women in the United States. By 1919, it had more than 20,000 members. Many of the WLAA volunteers were college students, with little experience of farm work. These "farmerettes" received the same pay as men. They shocked many who did not believe that women should work outdoors driving tractors, plowing fields, and wearing trousers! One member of the WLAA was asked whether the women would find the work too hard and return to the cities. She replied, "Would we quit? No, soldiers don't."

Horses were still used on farms in Europe, but many were sent to the Front to provide transportation.

TREATING THE WOUNDED

It was not just on the land or in the factories making boots, bombs, and bread that women had an impact. Just a few weeks after the start of the war, it was already clear that this would be a long and bloody conflict, and thousands of nurses would be needed to care for the wounded.

A Respectable Job

Nursing was one area of war that women had been involved with before. Florence Nightingale had led the way during the Crimean War of the 1850s. Nursing was seen as a more respectable job than working in a factory, and nurses were often young women from wealthier families, who volunteered because they wanted to help the war effort, rather than because they needed work to feed their families.

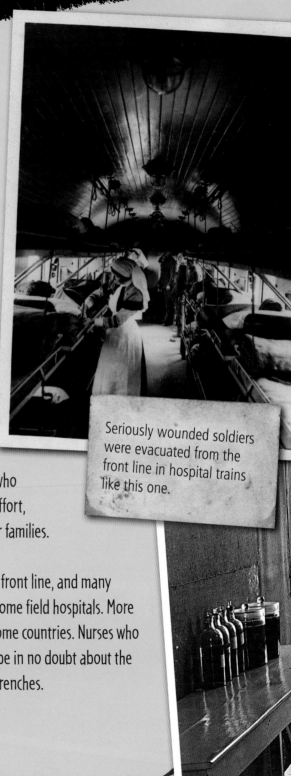

Seriously wounded soldiers were evacuated from the front line in hospital trains like this one.

Wounded soldiers were usually treated close to the front line, and many buildings in northern France were converted to become field hospitals. More serious injuries would lead to evacuation to their home countries. Nurses who treated the horrific wounds of these soldiers could be in no doubt about the terrible risks faced by their family members in the trenches.

Frontline Volunteers

Organizations such as the British Voluntary Aid Detachments had formed before the outbreak of war. The VADs were open to women and men, but most men volunteered or were drafted into the frontline forces. The VAD members worked as nurses and ambulance drivers close to the front line, where they faced the constant danger of being caught up in the fighting.

The National League for Woman's Service was the US equivalent of the VADs. The League filled many roles, including supplying trained radio operators. Just a few weeks after the United States joined the war in 1917, trained American nurses were on their way to Europe, before any US troops actually set sail. They set up field hospitals. By the end of the war, more than 21,000 nurses were enlisted in the US military, and around 10,000 of them were serving overseas.

Just like the troops themselves, hospital staff—like this Canadian nurse—often served far from home.

Women—working as nurses, on the land, in factories, offices, and elsewhere—played a vital part in the war effort on both sides. They did not usually fight in the trenches but, especially in the later years, women were able to join the military forces in support roles, such as cooking food and driving military vehicles.

Battalion of Death

The exception to this rule was the 1st Russian Women's Battalion of Death—the only female fighting force in the war. Maria Bochkareva, who had gained the Czar's permission to fight and was twice wounded, called for recruits at a time when Russia was going through revolution. About 2,000 women joined up.

There were other isolated examples of women on the front line, such as Dorothy Lawrence, who spent some time in the trenches disguised as a male soldier before being discovered.

Among the few women who served in the US forces were telephone operators who spoke French and English and were trained to use this new technology.

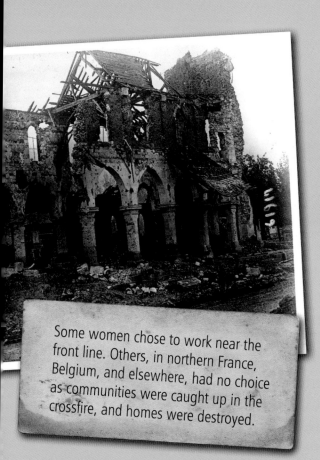

Some women chose to work near the front line. Others, in northern France, Belgium, and elsewhere, had no choice as communities were caught up in the crossfire, and homes were destroyed.

Supporting the Troops

Later in the war, governments needed to send every man they could to serve on the front line. Women took over many administrative roles. In Britain, the Women's Auxiliary Army Corps (WAAC) was set up in 1917. Members wore khaki uniforms and were organized in similar ranks to the regular army. The WAACs took on many support roles, including cooking, managing stores, driving trucks, and tending cemeteries. They were highly valued by the troops, not least because the food they prepared was said to be better than that of regular army cooks.

Primary Source: What Does It Tell Us?

American Frances Gulick worked as a volunteer cafeteria worker close to the Western Front during the war. Here she remembers how she felt when her parents visited her. What do her words tell you about how witnessing the war changed people's attitude to ordinary life?

"After the first thrill of the meeting, the presence of my parents in Gondrecourt gave me the queerest feeling. ...Home was incredibly remote. News of my friends with whom I had grown up seemed curiously flat and trivial. They lived in another world, which had ceased to concern me a great deal."

CHAPTER 4

FAMILIES AT HOME

Most adults were involved in the war—either fighting or supporting the efforts to win it. Even if they were not directly involved, the war changed the lives of families far from the front line.

World War I was one of the first "total wars." The countries involved had to use everything at their disposal, including industry, farming, and even the media, to secure victory. These economic tools were operated by civilians, so ordinary people found themselves in the firing line. Aircraft and other new weapons could reach farther than ever before.

Secondary Source: What Does It Tell Us?

News from the front line was heavily controlled. This story from a French hospital was published in a British newspaper in October 1914. Do you think it gives a full picture of what was really going on?

Cheerful Wounded

It was Sunday and therefore visiting day in the hospital. There were little groups around the bedsides of the French wounded —mothers, wives, and children. What a light-hearted courage the wounded have! As I entered one ward, there was a sound of singing. It came from the bed of the most cruelly injured man there.

A German family celebrates Christmas in the long period of relative peace in Europe before World War I.

A Changing World

Home life before the war was very different from modern life. Most of the technology we take for granted today either did not exist or was in its early stages. Automobiles had been around for a few years, but they were only just becoming affordable for ordinary people. The first airplanes flew just a few years before war broke out. The war was a time of changing technology and also big changes in society.

In order to organize and supply the military forces of the war, governments got more involved in people's lives than ever before. Industries such as railroads had to be controlled by governments to make sure they could transport troops effectively. Governments also tried to control what people heard and wrote about the war. Almost every area of life was more closely controlled than before the conflict.

The fighting on the Eastern Front destroyed many homes and villages.

FAMILIES UNDER ATTACK

Most armies did not set out to target civilians during the war, but powerful new weapons threatened families as never before. Families who lived in the conflict zones suffered most, as their homes were destroyed, and they were forced to flee. However, cities far from the front line faced air attacks during the war.

Crimes Against Civilians

Belgium was invaded by Germany at the start of the war. Britain and France spread many stories about crimes committed by German troops against the Belgians. Only some of these were true, but hundreds of thousands of Belgians did flee from the invaders. Around 250,000 of them took refuge in Britain. Other Belgians were forced to work in Germany. People in Poland and Serbia also suffered terribly from the fighting.

One of the greatest crimes against civilians in World War I took place in Turkey. Turkey's Armenian people were persecuted by their rulers and chose to side with Russian forces against them. Turkey's response was the murder of more than a million men, women, and children from the Armenian community.

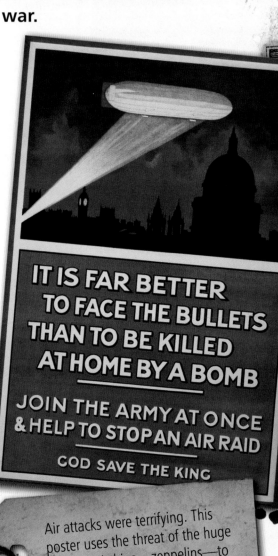

IT IS FAR BETTER TO FACE THE BULLETS THAN TO BE KILLED AT HOME BY A BOMB

JOIN THE ARMY AT ONCE & HELP TO STOP AN AIR RAID

GOD SAVE THE KING

Air attacks were terrifying. This poster uses the threat of the huge German airships—zeppelins—to persuade people to join the army.

Secondary Source: What Does It Tell Us?

The sinking of RMS *Lusitania* was a major shock to the United States, which was still a neutral country at the time. These are some of the newspaper headlines. What do the headlines tell you about how the sinking changed attitudes toward the war?

Liner *Lusitania* Sunk by German Submarine
(*Washington Times*)

Germany Glad Ship Sunk: 1,200 Die
(*El Paso Herald*)

Toll of *Lusitania* Victims Laid to German Murder Lust
(*Washington Herald*)

***Lusitania* Death Toll 1,346; 132 American Passengers Lost, Germany Jubilant**
(*Philadelphia Public Ledger*)

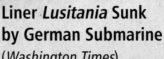

This stamp remembers the sinking of the *Lusitania*, which killed 1,198 civilians including more than 100 Americans.

Air and Sea Raids

Air attacks on civilians were a new and frightening feature of the war. Germany used zeppelins to attack cities such as Paris and London. As aircraft technology developed, fighters could defeat these slow-moving weapons. Later in the war, both sides used bomber aircraft, mainly in bombing industrial and military targets.

Merchant and passenger ships also faced attack by submarines. The most infamous was the sinking of the RMS *Lusitania* in May 1915. The outraged public in Britain and the United States believed this was unprovoked, but it was later discovered that the British liner had been carrying munitions for the Allies, just as Germany had claimed.

DEALING WITH SHORTAGES

The war put a great strain on food supplies in all the countries of Europe. This was partly because a lack of men and horses on the farms meant that crops were not planted and harvested efficiently. The fighting made some farmland unavailable, and blockades by warships and submarines prevented food arriving from overseas.

Families Starve

Women and children lining up for food became a common sight in many European cities. Germany and Austria-Hungary introduced rationing early in the war to make sure there was enough to go around. By the end of the war, thousands of people were starving in Central Europe. This was also the case in Russia, where the war stopped food from the south reaching the northern cities. Eventually, food shortages led to the revolution against the country's rulers in 1917.

Secondary Source: What Does It Tell Us?

This was one of many posters produced to encourage Americans to save food. How does the poster use words and images to convince people that they can make a difference?

"America the *hope* of all who suffer — the *dread* of all who wrong." WHITTIER

Save Food and defeat frightfulness
UNITED STATES FOOD ADMINISTRATION

In 1917, the British gov[ernment was] concerned that submarine attacks might lead to the country being starved out of the war. Merchant ships were organized into convoys to help them evade the U-boats.

Britain and France fared better due to good organization and to some imports getting through, despite the threat of submarine attack. The WLA and other schemes tried to grow as much as possible and helped produce more food. But they still had to introduce rationing later in the war.

"Food Will Win the War"

When the United States entered the war, President Woodrow Wilson set up the US Food Administration. Its job was to make sure there was enough food for American and Allied soldiers—and also for the people of the United States and her allies. They believed this could be achieved by encouraging people to eat less and not waste food. A campaign of posters and information reduced food consumption by 18 million tons (18.3 million tonnes), which could then be sent overseas.

CHILDREN DURING WARTIME

Children in wartime had to cope with shortages and the threat of attack, just as their parents did. Millions of boys and girls were forced to say goodbye to fathers and brothers who went to serve on the front line. They did not know if their loved ones would return, and many would lose a family member in the fighting. In Britain alone, more than 500,000 children had to grow up without fathers after theirs were killed in the war.

War at School

It was a war that children could not escape. It became part of their learning at school, where they would learn patriotic songs and hear about victories.

This poster encourages men to join the military because their children will be proud of them.

Daddy, what did YOU do in the Great War?

Primary Source: What Does It Tell Us?

This photo shows men from Kalamazoo, Michigan, leaving to fight in the war. One of them is carrying a girl, probably his daughter. She would not see her father for many months, or even years. What can you learn from this picture? How did people feel about the war? Do you think their feelings would have changed over time?

Children would not have heard much about the conditions in the trenches, or what was really happening in the war, although many would have known of soldiers who had been killed or wounded. Some textbooks from the time even show that the war was used as an example for math problems. Before 1917, the United States was neutral, and many families would have been supporting Germany. Once the United States had declared war, schools encouraged children to be patriotic and support US troops.

Young People Work for the War

Because their mothers were often working, older children were expected to spend more time looking after their younger brothers and sisters. Many teenagers were also working for the war. Children usually left school in their early teens and took jobs, including work in the munitions factories. Youth organizations such as the Boy Scouts and Girl Scouts raised money for the war.

Most information about the war came from newspapers and other printed information, such as posters. There were no TV or radio broadcasts, although some films of the war were shown in movie theaters. Public information was strictly controlled, and governments used propaganda to influence what people thought about the war. Letters home from the front line were also read—and censored if they revealed too much about what was happening in the trenches.

All Good News

Governments restricted the freedom of newspapers to print whatever they wanted. Officially, this was to keep sensitive information from reaching the enemy, but they also wanted to prevent too much bad news appearing, as this could destroy support for the war. Good news from the war was usually splashed all over the front page, while defeats might be hidden away on other pages.

Secondary Source: What Does It Tell Us?

This propaganda poster was produced in 1917. Who do you think this monster is supposed to represent? The goal of the poster was to show the enemy as brutal and less than human. Do you think the effect would be different if the image were more realistic?

Despite the losses and hardship during the war, there were few major protests against the war in most countries. Propaganda on both sides presented the war as a fight between good and evil. Organizations such as Britain's War Propaganda Bureau produced books, films, and posters supporting the war.

Committee of Public Information

US President Woodrow Wilson set up the Committee of Public information to organize publicity and propaganda for the US war effort. Its leader, George Creel, boasted, "There was no part of the great war machinery that we did not touch, no medium of appeal that we did not employ." Americans did not all support the war, and Creel used new techniques to convince people. He employed "four-minute men" to make short speeches in movie theaters to persuade people to buy war bonds. The United States also passed laws to prevent people openly criticizing the war.

The oldest daily newspaper published in the city of New Orleans. In continuous existence since September, 1827.

Published every morning except Monday in French and English, with an exclusively French newspaper issued weekly.

L'Abeille de la Nouvelle-Orléans.

POLITIQUE LITTERATURE   PRO ARIS ET FOCIS   SCIENCES ARTS

THE NEW ORLEANS BEE

VOLUME 89   THE NEW ORLEANS BEE, SATURDAY, APRIL 7, 1917.   NUMBER 277

SUITS INVOLVING MILLIONS ENDFD

ASKS CONGRESS TO DECLARE WAR

PRESIDENT TAKES VIGOROUS STEPS TO PROSECUTE THE WAR

IMPRISONNED IN HIS OWN PALACE

PEACE TALK RIFE IN SOME QUARTERS

Great Navy Ordered Mobilized and Volunteers Called for to Bring Army and National Guard to Full War Strength---Regulations for Aliens

In the United States, no publication that criticized the war could be sent through the mail, and offending publications were also removed from libraries.

CHAPTER 5

When the war began in 1914, many people had celebrated in the streets of Europe's cities. They believed the fighting would last only a few months. Very few people thought the war would last for more than four years and claim millions of lives. By the start of 1918, governments and military leaders were no longer predicting or planning a quick end to the war. Yet, in November 1918, the war ended. How did this happen?

Mutinies and Riots

By 1917, the two sides on the Western Front had been at a standstill for three years. Attacking the enemy's trenches directly led to very high casualties for the attackers. Shell explosions and rain churned up the landscape in which the armies fought. Governments also found it harder to hide the horrors of the fighting from the families back home. The catastrophic battles at Verdun and the Somme in 1916 had caused devastating loss of life on both sides. People were sick of war and, in 1917, there was a wave of

After four years of artillery bombardment and trench warfare, the fields of the Western Front had changed beyond all recognition.

Heinrich Beutow, a German schoolboy in 1917, remembers what people around him were saying about the war at that time. What do his words tell you about the mood in Germany and what people were thinking? Why were they not hopeful about the outcome of the war?

"There was a strong sense of people saying, "This war is lasting too long." Some people became quite outspoken. The feeling was that the war was lasting too long and that Germany didn't have much chance of winning it, because the conditions within the country were getting so very difficult."

mutinies in the French army, accompanied by strikes in French cities. In early 1918, there were also strikes and riots in Germany and Austria-Hungary.

Revolution in Russia

Russia's people suffered more than most from the shortages of the war, and their soldiers were very poorly equipped. In early March 1917, frustrations boiled over in a revolution that overthrew the Czar. In November 1917, the communist Bolsheviks took power. They soon started to agree to a peace treaty with Germany, so they could concentrate on fighting a civil war against their enemies at home. Germany could now focus on the Western Front, and things looked bleak for the Allies.

Lenin was the leader of the Bolshevik government in Russia. He promised to end the war, but Russia's exhausted people then had to face a brutal civil war.

The Germans seemed to have a small advantage at the beginning of 1918, but in the long term the balance of power would change decisively, and the Germans knew it. This was partly a result of US troops joining the fight, but was also due to the organization and efforts of men, women, and children on the home fronts.

Machine gun practice - Camp Sherman,   Chillicothe, Ohio.

Inexperienced but fresh US soldiers, called "doughboys," turned the tide in 1918.

Desperate Last Fights

When US troops arrived in France in spring 1918, the armies that had been fighting since 1914 were running out of soldiers. Germany and Austria-Hungary knew that 1918 was their last chance to win the war, and they launched a desperate offensive in March 1918. For several weeks they pushed French and British forces back deep into France. However, in July of that year, the Western Allies—now boosted by half a million US soldiers—began to fight back. The Germans were exhausted and had few reserves to call on. Meanwhile, the Allies were going from strength to strength. By November, the number of US troops on the Western Front had risen to around two million.

The Allies Win

The Allies were also winning the war on the home front. Their factories were producing more tanks, aircraft, and shells. Families might have complained about rationing in Britain and France,

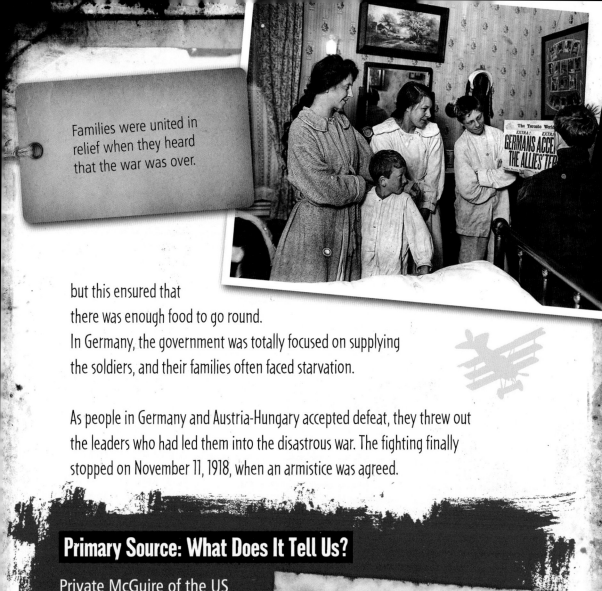

Families were united in relief when they heard that the war was over.

but this ensured that there was enough food to go round. In Germany, the government was totally focused on supplying the soldiers, and their families often faced starvation.

As people in Germany and Austria-Hungary accepted defeat, they threw out the leaders who had led them into the disastrous war. The fighting finally stopped on November 11, 1918, when an armistice was agreed.

Primary Source: What Does It Tell Us?

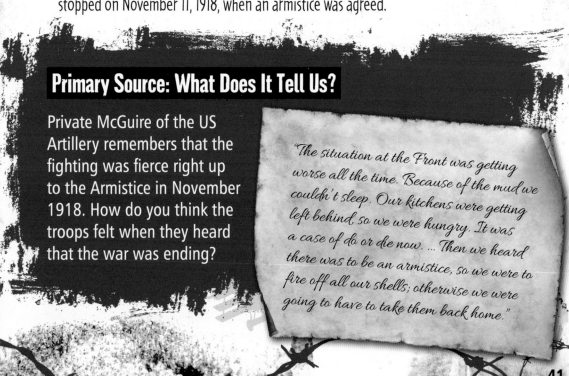

Private McGuire of the US Artillery remembers that the fighting was fierce right up to the Armistice in November 1918. How do you think the troops felt when they heard that the war was ending?

"The situation at the Front was getting worse all the time. Because of the mud we couldn't sleep. Our kitchens were getting left behind, so we were hungry. It was a case of do or die now. ... Then we heard there was to be an armistice, so we were to fire off all our shells; otherwise we were going to have to take them back home."

CHAPTER 6

RECOVERY AND REMEMBRANCE

When World War I finally ended, Europe was in chaos. Some countries, such as Russia and Germany, were shaken by revolution. Others had to adjust to the huge human and financial cost of the war.

Soldiers and civilians celebrated the end of the war.

The Dead and Wounded

In the months following the war, people began to count the cost. Around 10 million soldiers had died in the war, leaving families without fathers, sons, and brothers. The death toll of civilians from enemy attack, starvation, and other crimes such as the Armenian massacres, was probably just as great. Many millions of soldiers were wounded in the war, having to continue life without legs and arms, or with mental scars from their experiences of war. Many of them were totally changed from the people who had gone to war in 1914.

Hundreds of thousands of victims of the Western Front are remembered in cemeteries like this, in northern France and Belgium.

Flu Follows War

Immediately after the war a disease known as Spanish Flu swept across the world, carried by soldiers returning from Europe. It claimed more lives than the war itself, especially in the United States, where the epidemic killed 550,000 people, in addition to the 50,000 Americans who died in battle.

Achievements and Sacrifice

In those countries that did not immediately erupt in revolution, political leaders vowed to create a new world from the disaster of World War I. In Britain, all adult men were allowed to vote in elections for the first time. Women had campaigned for the vote before the war. After the war, they finally achieved their goal in many countries, including Great Britain–where women over 30 were trusted with the vote–the United States, Canada, Germany, and elsewhere.

Families in all the warring nations set out to remember the dead. In many cases, local communities donated money to erect war memorials to record those who did not return. Their sacrifice is still remembered every year on November 11, known as Veterans Day in the United States.

Many of the bodies from the battlefields of World War I could not be identified. The Tomb of the Unknown Soldier in Arlington, Virginia, remembers the American victims. There are similar tombs in many cities around the world.

A NEW WORLD

Having to live without loved ones was just one of the ways in which the world changed for many families after 1918. The years after the war were difficult times, with many of those who had fought in the war facing economic problems and unemployment. There were, however, some benefits, such as medical advances made during the war.

Problems After the War

Soldiers returning from the war wanted to go straight back to their old jobs, but things were not always so simple. Industries such as shipbuilding and steelmaking had been boosted by the demand during wartime. This did not continue after the war, and there was widespread

Adolf Hitler fought and was injured in World War I. He then went on to rise to power in Germany, and his actions triggered World War II.

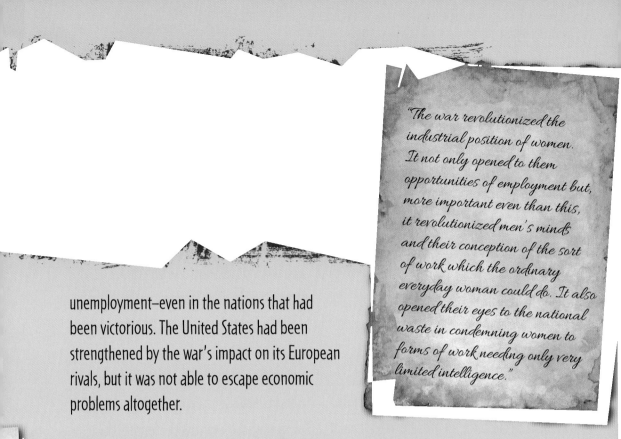

"The war revolutionized the industrial position of women. It not only opened to them opportunities of employment but, more important even than this, it revolutionized men's minds and their conception of the sort of work which the ordinary everyday woman could do. It also opened their eyes to the national waste in condemning women to forms of work needing only very limited intelligence."

unemployment—even in the nations that had been victorious. The United States had been strengthened by the war's impact on its European rivals, but it was not able to escape economic problems altogether.

During the war, women proved that they could handle many jobs and responsibilities that had been closed to them before. Although some of these gains were lasting, many women found themselves out of a job when male workers returned from the war.

A Peaceful Future?

The families who emerged from the war hoped that their children would never have to experience anything like it. Many people also wanted to punish Germany for starting the war. At the peace conference after the war, the victorious countries demanded crippling compensation payments from Germany and redrew the map of Europe, reducing Germany's territory. Instead of creating lasting peace, this treaty prepared the ground for a strong leader to emerge, promising he would make Germany great again. Just 20 years later, Adolf Hitler would plunge the planet into a second world war, more terrible than the first.

armistice agreement to stop fighting a war

artillery large guns for long-distance fighting

assassination killing of someone, usually for political reasons

casualties people who are hurt or killed

censored restricted access to information, such as by controlling what newspapers print

colonies lands ruled by the government of another country

communist person or group who believes in creating an equal society through government control of property and many other areas of life

conscription forcing all men between certain ages to serve in the military

Eastern Front in the war, the border between land controlled by Germany and Austria-Hungary and that controlled by Russia

evacuated moved people away from a location

khaki brown color used in military uniforms

labor unions organizations of workers formed to campaign for rights from their employers

mobilize prepare armies for war

munitions weapons, ammunition, and other supplies needed to make war

mutinies when groups of people rise up, refuse orders, and try to take control

nationalist a person from a political group that strongly campaigns for national independence

neutral not favoring one side or the other

Ottoman Empire lands controlled from what is now Turkey, including large areas of the Middle East in 1914

patriotic strongly supporting your country

persecuted targeted or discriminated against

propaganda information designed by a government or organization to promote a particular message

rationing restricting how much food and other items people can buy to ensure there is enough for everyone

shells explosives fired from an artillery gun

Western Front border between the land controlled by Germany and the Western Allies in World War I, where heavy fighting took place

zeppelin giant gas-filled airship, used by the Germans as a bomber in the war

Books

Adams, Simon. *World War I* (Eyewitness Books). New York, NY: DK, 2007.

Hunter, Nick. *Women in World War I* (Remembering World War 1). Chicago, IL: Heinemann-Raintree, 2013.

Perritano, John. *World War I* (America at War). New York, NY: Scholastic, 2010.

Swain, Gwenyth. *World War I: An Interactive History Adventure* (You Choose: History). Mankato, MN: Capstone, 2012.

Websites

Learn more with this multimedia review of the war:
www.firstworldwar.com

Visit the United States' National World War I Museum in Kansas City, MO:
theworldwar.org

The Imperial War Museum in London, England, has an enormous collection of resources about World War I. Take a look here:
www.iwm.org.uk

Publisher's note to educators and parents: Our editors have carefully reviewed these websites to ensure that they are suitable for students. Many websites change frequently, however, and we cannot guarantee that a site's future contents will continue to meet our high standards of quality and educational value. Be advised that students should be closely supervised whenever they access the Internet.